ENGLISH LANGUAGE AND PUNCTUATION BOOKLET

Keith Williams

WILLIAMS
DYFFRYN ARDUDWY   GWYNEDD

© *Keith Williams, 2015*
First published in Great Britain, 2015
All rights reserved.
No part of this publication may be reproduced or transmitted in any form or by any means, electronic or mechanical, including photocopy, recording, or any information storage and retrieval system, without permission in writing from the copyright holder.

British Library Cataloguing-in-Publication Data.
A catalogue record for this book is available from the British Library.

ISBN 978-0-9933299-0-6
Printed in Great Britain by
Arthur H. Stockwell Ltd
Torrs Park   Ilfracombe
Devon EX34 8BA

ENGLISH LANGUAGE

AN EASIER WAY

This self-study pack is intended to provide *an easier way* to improve the reader's spoken and written English language by means of the study of 125 sentences featuring a mix of common and less-known errors and their correction.

The pack includes:
- Sentences in which errors are featured;
- Simple explanations of the errors;
- Sentences providing correction of the errors.

For the learning process to be effective, it is recommended that any inclination on the part of the reader to hurry through the total pack be resisted.

The study of one unit per week is considered to be the most effective way to achieve full understanding, which can be expected to result in the reader's subsequent adoption of the correct versions automatically.

Repeated reference to the unit for the week will ensure this correct usage, which will be reinforced by recognition of the errors when made by others, especially by individuals, such as announcers and celebrities on television, who are expected to have a good command of the language, and by performers in the 'soaps' who are not.

UNIT 1: ADJECTIVES AND ADVERBS

To be corrected:
1. I can run as quick as my dog.
2. You must drive quicker if you don't want to be late.
3. At least he is thinking positive after losing the game.
4. It was great to see you yesterday.
5. You played good in the match last Saturday.
6. Going for a walk is equally as good as playing sport for keeping fit.
7. I had hardly started than I was interrupted.

Relevant Notes:
Adjectives are words used to **describe** nouns.
Nouns are words used to **refer** to places, persons and objects.
Adverbs are used to **qualify** verbs.
Verbs are words used to **signify** an action or a state.

Explanations of the errors:
Sentence No. 1
The word '**run**' is a verb, because it signifies action and the word '**quick**' is an adjective. Therefore, there is a mismatch. What is required to **qualify** the word '**run**' is a word that describes how '**I can run**'. The word '**quick**' needs to be turned into an adverb and to do that

we add '**ly**' and make it '**quickly**'.

Many adjectives are converted into adverbs in this way, but many are not and need to be learned over time. Examples of such adverbs are: '**soon**' and '**well**'.

Sentence No. 2
The word '**quicker**' is an adjective, and is used here incorrectly to **qualify** the verb '**drive**'. An adverb is needed so '**quicker**' converts to '**more quickly**'.

Sentence No. 3
The incorrect manner in which the adjective '**positive**' is used here is the error and, indeed, this particular word has crept into common usage in recent years with linkage to unsuitable verbs, as is the case in this sentence. '**Positive**' has several meanings with '**certain**' being until recent times its most popular usage. In this sentence it means '**acknowledge that all is not lost, because there are promising signs to take comfort from**'.

This indicates the unsuitability of the verb and the need for it to be replaced by '**being**' or the change from '**is being positive**' to '**is positive**'.

Sentence No. 4
The use of the word '**great**' is hardly appropriate here. More appropriate would be '**nice**' or simply '**good**'.

Sentence No. 5
The use of '**good**' is incorrect, because an adverb is needed to **qualify** the verb '**played**' and '**good**' is an adjective. An appropriate choice here is '**well**'.

Sentence No. 6
The mistake here is the use of '**as**' following the adverb '**equally**'. The correct version is '**equally good as . . .**'.

Sentence No. 7

The word '**hardly**' is not the adverb of the adjective '**hard**'. Somewhat strangely the adverb of the adjective '**hard**' is the same word '**hard**'.

The word '**hardly**' means '**scarcely**' and is followed by the adverb '**when**' not by '**than**' in correct English.

The revised versions of the sentences:
1. I can run as quickly as my dog.
2. You must drive more quickly if you don't want to be late.
3. At least he is positive after losing the game.
4. It was nice to see you yesterday.
5. You played well in the match last Saturday.
6. Going for a walk is equally good as playing sport for keeping fit.
7. I had hardly started when I was interrupted.

Now, go back to the original sentences and write them correctly without reference to these revised versions.

UNIT 2: COMPARATIVES AND SUPERLATIVES

To be corrected:
1. He is the most able of her parents.
2. I am the less likely of the three of us to be late for work.
3. There are less people here than I expected.
4. Losing my job is the worst of the two main concerns I have at the present time.
5. Sunday will be the best day of the weekend.
6. Of his brothers he was the most gifted when they were young.
7. Compared to the thirties, when I was a child, more of the children today are less fit.

Relevant Notes:
Consider the differences between the following versions of **comparatives** and **superlatives** in respect of adjectives:
- Whilst he is a **good** boy, his brother, John, is a **better** boy and the other brother, James, is the **best** of the three of them.
- The word '**better**' is the **comparative** of the word '**good**' and '**best**' is the **superlative**.
- Whilst he was a **bad** boy, his brother, John, was **worse** and the other brother, James, was the **worst** of the three.
    The word '**worse**' is the **comparative** of the word

'**bad**' and '**worst**' is the **superlative**.
- There are **few** people here today, but there were **fewer** yesterday and tomorrow we expect the **fewest** number of people to come here this week.

    The words '**fewer**' and '**fewest**' are the **comparative** and **superlative** forms, respectively, of the word '**few**'.
- He is **careful** when he washes the dishes, but his sister is even **more careful** and their mother is the **most careful** of the three of them.

In short, then, there are some adjectives which have special words for their **comparatives** and **superlatives**, whilst others need the use of '**more**' and '**most**', as illustrated above.

Consider now **comparatives** and **superlatives** for adverbs, as follows:
- He is walking **well** for a child as young as he is, but at the same age his sister walked even **better** and their cousin walked **best** of the three of them at that age.
- He is walking **badly** for a child of his age, but at the same age his sister walked even **worse** and their cousin walked **worst** of the three of them.

Note that the **comparative** and **superlative** forms of the adjective '**good**' and the adverb '**well**' are the same.

Further examples of the **comparative** and **superlative** forms of adverbs are as follows:
- He walks **slowly**, but his friend walks even **more slowly** and I walk **most slowly** of all.
- She sings **beautifully**, but I must admit that he sings **more beautifully** and the choir sings **most beautifully** of all.

Explanations of the errors:
Sentence No. 1
He, obviously, would have **two** parents, not **three or more** as the word '**most**' suggests. Therefore, the word '**more**' is needed, instead of '**most**'.

Sentence No. 2
'**Less likely . . .**' would be correct for **two**, but there are **three**. The word '**least**' is needed, instead of '**less**'.

Sentence No 3
The incorrect word is '**less**' and needs to be replaced by '**fewer**'. This is a very common error and one to be mastered.

Sentence No. 4
He had **two** main concerns, which means that the word '**worst**' is an incorrect choice. The **superlative** of '**bad**' has been used when the **comparative** form was required. Thus, the correct word to be inserted here is '**worse**'.

Sentence No. 5
There are **two** days on a weekend. This means that the word '**best**' is incorrect and should be '**better**'.

Sentence No. 6
The error here is his inclusion with the brothers such that he became a brother of himself. He cannot be his own brother.

Sentence No. 7
The sentence structure is poor and results in '**Compared to . . .**' being misrelated to '**more of the children . . .**' Misrelated parts of a sentence will be discussed more fully in a later section of the pack.

The revised versions of the sentences:
1. He is the more able of her parents.
2. I am the least likely of the three of us to be late for work.
3. There are fewer people here than I expected.
4. Losing my job is the worse of the two main concerns I have at the present time.
5. Sunday will be the better day of the weekend.
6. When they were young, he was more gifted than his brothers.
7. Compared to the thirties, when I was a child, today, more children are not so fit.

Now, go back to the original sentences and write them correctly without reference to these revised versions.

UNIT 3: WHO/WHOM/WHOSE/WHOEVER/WHOMEVER

To be corrected:
1. For the benefit of who are we collecting money?
2. He described the person whom, he said, was responsible for the road accident.
3. To who does this penknife belong?
4. I'll choose whoever I like to be my partner.
5. The picture on the wall is of a relative who nobody in the family seems to remember.
6. If you break the law, you will get into trouble whomever you are.
7. In the presence of who are we in this meeting today?

Relevant Notes:
To differentiate between '**who**' and '**whom**', it is merely necessary to respect that '**who**' is the **subject** of the verb and '**whom**' is the **object**.

Consider: The cat is chasing the mouse.
- In this sentence '**The cat**' is the **subject** and '**the mouse**' is the **object**.

Not identifying correctly the **subject** of a sentence is a common fault in spoken and written English and is, thereby, the reason for confusion with an **object** and/or other characteristics of the sentence.

Using '**who**' and '**whom**' correctly is a good way of overcoming this particular difficulty.

Explanations of the errors:
Sentence No. 1
Firstly, turn the sentence round so that it becomes easier to spot the **subject**. This results in:
   We are collecting this money for the benefit of who?
   Clearly, the subject is '**We**' and the fact that in the original sentence it did not appear first is not relevant. The **subject** of a sentence can appear at any point in a sentence, particularly if it is a question.
   Moreover, we cannot say '**of who**', and, indeed, we cannot use the word '**who**' after the following: '**by**', '**with**', '**of**', '**from**', '**for**', '**to**' or '**on**'. Whenever one of these **prepositions** is used in front of '**who**' it is necessary to change the word to '**whom**'.

Sentence No. 2
Here we have to recognise that the word '**whom**' is the **subject** of the verb '**was**' and must be changed to '**who**', accordingly.

Sentence No. 3
As mentioned above, following '**to**' we cannot use '**who**' which needs to be changed to '**whom**'. Generally, however, the structure used in this instance is: '**Whose penknife is this?**'

Sentence No. 4
The word '**whoever**' is used in the same way as '**who**' and, in this sentence is the **object** of the verb '**choose**' so it needs to be changed to '**whomever**'.

Sentence No. 5
The word '**who**' is incorrect, because it relates to the phrase '**nobody ... seems to remember**' and is the **object** of it. So, it needs to become '**whom**'.

Sentence No. 6
The word '**whomever**' relates to '**you**' which is the **subject** of the verb '**are**' and, therefore, needs to change to '**whoever**'.

Sentence No. 7
The word '**who**' follows '**of**' and must be changed to '**whom**'.

The revised versions of the sentences:
1. For the benefit of whom are we collecting money?
2. He described the person who, he said, was responsible for the road accident.
3. Whose penknife is this?
4. I'll choose whomever I like to be my partner.
5. The picture on the wall is of a relative whom nobody in the family seems to remember.
6. If you break the law, you will get into trouble whoever you are.
7. In the presence of whom are we in this meeting today?

Now, go back to the original sentences and write them correctly without reference to these revised versions.

UNIT 4: MAY/MIGHT/CAN/COULD

To be corrected:
1. He may not have intended to be rude.
2. I might go shopping on Friday.
3. That might be so, but I'm not convinced.
4. You can do that since you really want to.
5. He could well come back at any moment.
6. You might find that you are able to do it if you try.
7. I could of given you a few minutes of my time.
8. Try as they might, the police cannot prevent some drivers from exceeding the speed limit.
9. Studying hard at college might benefit you in the future.

Relevant Notes:
- Whilst the words '**may**' and '**might**' are used as though they are interchangeable, there is a distinction, which is rarely respected, mainly because, apparently, most people are unaware of it.
- The rule is: '**may**' is used in the **present** and **future** tenses, whilst '**might**' is used in the **past** tense.

Consider, therefore: I '**might**' have gone yesterday, but I decided not to, and now I '**may**' go today, but, instead, I '**may**' go next Thursday.

Note, however, that '**might**' is very commonly used in the **future** tense to the extent that this practice has become acceptable.

Thus, '**I might be there tomorrow**', is more likely to be heard than '**I may be there tomorrow**'.

'**Might**' has another, very different meaning, which is a peculiarity of the English language; this being that it means also **power** or **strength**.

Examples of this usage are:

- He tried with all his **might** to get me to change my mind.
- I tried with all my **might** to remove the cork from the bottle, without success.

The word '**can**' from the verb '**to be able**' is used often instead of '**may**' to mean precisely the same. In such cases it is better that '**may**' be used instead.

The word '**could**' is also from the verb '**to be able**' and a fairly common error is for '**could have**', in the **past** tense, to be written and spoken as '**could of**'. This is a poor error!

The word '**might**' is often used instead of '**could**' in complaints such as: '**you might have helped me with the chores**'.

Explanations of the errors:
Sentence No. 1
Because of the rule explained earlier, the word '**might**' is more suitable here than '**may**'.

Sentence No. 2
Again, because of the rule, the word '**may**' is a better choice than '**might**'.

Sentence No. 3
Yet again the word '**might**' is not a good choice for the reasons already stated. So, it is changed to '**may**'.

Sentence No. 4
Whilst the word '**can**' is commonly used, it is more correct to use '**may**' here.

Sentence No. 5
Although '**could**' is commonly used in this structure, it is more correct to use '**may**'.

Sentence No. 6
The word '**may**' is better than '**might**'.

Sentence No. 7
The phrase '**could of**' is incorrect and needs to be changed to '**could have**'.

Sentence No. 8
The word '**might**' should be changed to '**may**'.

Sentence No. 9
The word '**might**' should be changed to '**may**'.

The revised versions of the sentences:
1. He might not have intended to be rude.
2. I may go shopping on Friday.
3. That may be so, but I'm not convinced.
4. You may do that since you really want to.
5. He may well come back at any moment.

6. You may find that you are able to do it if you try.
7. I could have given you a few minutes of my time.
8. Try as they may, the police cannot prevent some drivers from exceeding the speed limit.
9. Studying hard at college may benefit you in the future.

Now, go back to the original sentences and write them correctly without reference to these revised versions.

UNIT 5: EVERYBODY/EVERYONE/ANYONE/ANY

To be corrected:
1. Everybody should take care of their credit cards when shopping in this store.
2. I don't know anyone who write cheques today instead of using credit or debit cards.
3. Anyone who admits stealing the money will not be reported to the police.
4. He invited everyone to bring their children to the Christmas party.
5. Any new members of the club cannot use the facilities during the first month of their membership.
6. Everybody should be concerned about guarding their health.
7. Everybody is shopping at Aldi now.

Relevant Notes:
'**Everyone**', '**anyone**', and '**everybody**' are words that refer to **one person only** and, yet, too often they are used to refer to people in the plural.

Consider the following: '**Everybody**' must do their best.

A difficulty here is that the plural may include both

sexes and a more correct version is cumbersome, as the following shows: '**Everybody**' must do his or her best. A simple alternative is: All people must do their best.

Consider another example: '**Everybody**' must leave their valuables in the safe.

Alternative, correct, versions: All valuables must be left in the safe. Valuables must be left in the safe.

Another problem arising from the use of '**everybody**' is that it can incur exaggeration as the following illustrates: '**Everybody**' is going on holiday by air these days.

This claim is, of course, completely untrue, but it typifies the sort of headline that we encounter in newspapers.

It is incorrect to use the words '**anyone**' and '**any**' in a negative sentence.

Explanations of the errors:
Sentence No. 1
The word '**everybody**' is misrelated to '**their**'.
   An alternative, correct sentence is: Customers must take care of their credit cards when shopping in this store.

Sentence No. 2
The word '**anyone**' is singular, which means that '**write**' must be changed to '**writes**'.

Sentence No. 3
The word '**anyone**' cannot be used in conjunction with '**not**'.

Sentence No. 4
The word '**everybody**' is singular and, therefore, does not agree with '**their**'.

Sentence No. 5
The word '**any**' cannot be followed by a negative verb.

Sentence No. 6
The problem here is the use of the word '**everybody**' in relation to '**their**'. Switching the sentence round is an effective way of overcoming the problem.
 One alternative is as follows: Guarding one's health should be the concern of '**everybody**'.

Sentence No. 7
This is an example of gross exaggeration and could have been featured in a newspaper.

The revised versions of the sentences:
1. Customers must take care of their credit cards when shopping in this store.
2. I don't know anyone who writes cheques today instead of using credit or debit cards.
3. Nobody who admits stealing the money will be reported to the police.
4. He invited all parents to bring their children to the Christmas party.
5. No new members of the club can use the facilities during the first month of their membership.
6. Guarding one's health should be the concern of everybody.
7. Aldi is experiencing increasing popularity with shoppers.

Now, go back to the original sentences and write them correctly without reference to these revised versions.

UNIT 6: NEGATION/NONE/NOBODY

To be corrected:
1. I don't know nothing about him.
2. All the children are not badly behaved.
3. He is not going to come, I don't think.
4. I am not blaming no one for my accident.
5. Several candidates were interviewed, but none were suitable for the job.
6. I shall have nothing to do with him no more.
7. Just as I don't like cabbage, nor do I like sprouts.
8. Nobody wants to lose their way in the dark.
9. None of my friends are overweight.
10. I didn't recognise none of the guests there.
11. I have two sisters and neither agree with me.

Relevant Notes:
Double negatives, as included in many of the sentences to be corrected, are very common mistakes in English, which, to some extent, is excusable, because in some other languages they are used as a normal and proper grammatical feature.

Explanations of the errors:
Sentence No. 1
The word **'don't'** is a contraction of **'do not'** and,

therefore, there is a **double negative** in this sentence, being '**not**' and '**nothing**'. We have a choice when it comes to making the correction.

Either '**don't**' is deleted or '**nothing**' is changed to '**anything**'.

Sentence No. 2
This sentence is not incorrect in terms of the words featured. It is, however, included here to serve as an example of how the way a sentence is spoken influences the meaning conveyed and how word order can cause confusion over the meaning of the written sentence.

If, when the sentence is spoken, there is emphasis on the word '**All**' the meaning conveyed is that **some are badly behaved, but not all**.

As it stands the written version can mean either no children are badly behaved or some only are badly behaved.

Therefore, to remove ambiguity, the sentence needs to be reworded.

Sentence No. 3
The attachment of '**I don't think**' to a negative statement is quite common and produces a **double negative**.

The alternative corrections are as follows:

a) I don't think he's going to come.
b) I think he's not going to come.
c) He is not going to come, I think.

Sentence No. 4
This sentence also features a **double negative**, being '**not**' and '**no one**'. The correction is to change '**no one**' to '**anyone**'.

Sentence No. 5
The error here is the use of the plural verb '**were**' for a singular **subject** '**none**'. The correction is to change the verb to '**was**'.

Sentence No. 6
The **double negative** arises from '**nothing**' and '**no more**'. The solution is to change '**no more**' to '**any more**'.

Sentence No. 7
This sentence is badly worded and suffers from the use of '**just as**'. Whilst technically the use of '**neither**' instead of '**nor**' will improve the grammar, the rephrasing to avoid the use of '**just as**' is recommended.
The following is better wording: I like neither cabbage nor sprouts.
The alternative is: I don't like either cabbage or sprouts.

Sentence No. 8
The error is the use of the singular '**nobody**' in relation to the plural '**their**'. The correction is to change '**their**' to '**his or her**', which, although it is clumsy wording, is correct English.

Sentence No. 9
The error is the use of '**are**' when the **subject** of the verb is singular, being '**None**'.

Sentence No. 10
The word '**none**' is incorrect and needs to be changed to '**any**'.

Sentence No. 11
The word '**neither**' requires a singular verb, which means that '**agree**' must be changed to '**agrees**'.

The revised versions of the sentences:
1. I don't know anything about him.
2. Not all the children are badly behaved.
3. I think he is not going to come.
4. I'm not blaming anyone for my accident.
5. Several candidates were interviewed, but none was suitable for the job.
6. I shall have nothing to do with him any more.
7. I like neither cabbage nor sprouts.
8. Nobody wants to lose his or her way in the dark.
9. None of my friends is overweight.
10. I didn't recognise any of the guests there.
11. I have two sisters and neither agrees with me.

Now, go back to the original sentences and write them correctly without reference to these revised versions.

UNIT 7: PRONOUNS

To be corrected:
1. He invited John and I to the ceremony.
2. Him coming to the funeral pleased me very much.
3. David is a better husband than me.
4. Me and my wife went shopping this morning.
5. He is as keen as me to win the game.
6. John, Wendy and myself are going to the theatre this evening.
7. Both her and my mother like to visit their friends in the countryside.
8. The car standing on the drive is our's.
9. It was him who was to blame.
10. The other women were more excited about the new baby than her.
11. Me being to blame is absurd.
12. He is used to them being on the radio.

Relevant Notes:
Pronouns are words used in place of **nouns** and take different forms.
Personal pronouns are: '**I**' and '**me**', '**he**' and '**him**', '**she**' and '**her**' etc.
Demonstrative pronouns are: '**this**', '**that**', '**these**' and '**those**'.

Interrogative pronouns are: '**who**', '**which**', '**that**' and '**what**'.

Problems arise from a failure, sometimes, to respect that '**I**', '**he**', '**she**', '**we**' and '**they**' are **subjects** of verbs and '**me**', '**him**', '**her**', '**us**' and '**them**' are **objects** of verbs. '**You**' functions as either **subject** or **object**, as required.

The verb '**to be**' causes problems, as the selected sentences for correction will illustrate.

Explanations of the errors:
Sentence No. 1
'**I**' must be changed to '**me**' because it is, with John, the **object** of the verb '**invited**'.

Sentence No. 2
'**Him**' is incorrect, because it is being used here to describe the word '**coming**' which is a participle requiring, in this case, a **possessive pronoun**. The word required is '**His**'.

Today, this type of pronoun is being described, somewhat surprisingly, as a **possessive adjective**.

The other **possessives** in this category are, of course, '**my**', '**her**', '**our**', '**your**', and '**their**'.

Sentence No. 3
'**Me**' needs to be changed to '**I**'.

There is a useful rule to be applied in this type of grammatical structure. This states that: If a verb cannot be added sensibly '**me**' is incorrect and must be changed to '**I**'.

Use of the rule reveals that the correct word in this case is '**I**'.

Consider, then, the sentence: Sheila is a better wife than '**her**'.

This is incorrect and needs to be changed to: Sheila is a better wife than '**she**'.

This is because a verb cannot be sensibly added, in this case, to '**her**'; whereas, the word '**is**' can be added to '**she**'.

Sentence No. 4
Correction is needed to the **subject** of the verb '**went**'. So, '**Me and my wife**' changes to '**My wife and I**'.

Sentence No. 5
The rule described earlier and applied to Sentence No. 3 is applicable here also and causes change from '**me**' to '**I**'.

Sentence No. 6
The word '**myself**' is incorrect in that it is not a **subject pronoun**. The **subject** of the verb '**are going**' needs to be changed to '**John, Wendy and I**'.

Sentence No. 7
The word '**her**' needs to be changed to '**she**' and the word '**Both**' is misplaced in the sentence. Incorrect **word order** is a common fault and is illustrated well in this sentence.

The revised start to this sentence is: '**She and my mother both went . . .**'

Sentence No. 8
The error here is the insertion of the apostrophe.

Sentence No. 9
The word '**him**' is incorrect. The use of the verb '**to be**' determines that the **subject** of '**him**' be used and, therefore, '**he**' is to be used instead.

Sentence No. 10
Again the rule quoted earlier may be employed here to show that '**her**' is incorrect and needs to be changed to '**she**'.

Sentence No. 11
The word '**Me**' is incorrect and '**My**' is required to replace it, because it describes the participle '**being**'.

Sentence No. 12
The word '**them**' is incorrect and constitutes the same type of error as was featured in Sentence No. 11. So, '**them**' changes to '**their**'.

The revised versions of the sentences:
1. He invited John and me to the ceremony.
2. His coming to the funeral pleased me very much.
3. David is a better husband than I.
4. My wife and I went shopping this morning.
5. He is as keen as I to win the game.
6. John, Wendy and I are going to the theatre this evening.
7. She and my mother both like to visit their friends in the countryside.
8. The car standing on the drive is ours.
9. It was he who was to blame.
10. The other women were more excited about the new baby than she.
11. My being to blame is absurd.
12. He is used to their being on the radio.

Now, go back to the original sentences and write them correctly without reference to these revised versions.

UNIT 8: COLLECTIVE NOUNS

To be corrected:
1. A committee was formed, but they couldn't reach a decision on the first issue they discussed.
2. Last Saturday, although the team played well, the result was a big disappointment for the players.
3. A large flock of geese flew above us and, then, they came down to feed on my vegetable patch.
4. It was a large audience for the first night of the play and their applause showed how much they enjoyed the performance.
5. The family was invited to the wedding, but they didn't all come to the church.
6. A meeting of the office staff was held and they discussed the offer of the poor pay rise very angrily.
7. There is a pride of lions at the zoo and I recommend you go and see them.

Relevant Notes:
A **collective noun** is in singular form, but the complication in using it is the fact that it refers to a **group of things or individuals**.

It is important to take care to ensure that a sentence,

written or spoken, does not incorporate both the singular and group characteristics.

This fault occurs in all seven sentences.

Explanations of the errors:
Sentence No.1
The committee is singular, but the members of it are expressed in the plural.

The most obvious correction is to change '**they**', which occurs twice, to '**it**' on each occasion.

Sentence No. 2
Similarly, the singular form of '**team**' is mismatched with '**players**'.

Choices for its correction are either to change '**the players**' to '**it**' or to insert the word '**all**' before '**the team**'. The use of '**all**' would have the effect of pluralising the word '**team**'.

Sentence No. 3
The mismatch here is between '**a large flock**' and '**they**'. The simple correction is the alteration of '**they**' to '**it**'.

Sentence No. 4
The word '**their**' should be '**its**' and '**they**' changes to '**it**'.

Sentence No. 5
There are two options for correction here. One is to change '**was**' to '**were**' and insert the word '**All**' before '**the family**'; the other is to change '**they . . . all**' to '**it**'. Of the two choices, the first seems to be the better.

Sentence No. 6

The adjustment needed here is to change 'they' to 'it', which serves to maintain the singular characteristic of the staff.

Sentence No. 7

The simple correction is to change 'them' to 'it'.

The revised versions of the sentences:
1. A committee was formed, but it couldn't reach a decision on the very first issue it discussed.
2. Last Saturday, although all the team played well, the result was a big disappointment for the players.
3. A large flock of geese flew above us and, then, it came down to feed on my vegetable patch.
4. It was a large audience for the first night of the play and its applause showed how much it enjoyed the performance.
5. All the family were invited to the wedding, but they didn't all come to the church.
6. A meeting of the office staff was held and it discussed the offer of a poor pay rise very angrily.
7. There is a pride of lions at the zoo and I recommend you go and see it.

Now, go back to the original sentences and write them correctly without reference to these revised versions.

UNIT 9: MISRELATED

To be corrected:
1. Having told you that the weather will be bad today, it hasn't rained at all yet and it's mid-afternoon now.
2. Thinking about the economic situation, the UK must export more to help us to clear the deficit.
3. Having said that, the best thing we can do is stay here until it stops raining.
4. Last week, whilst driving, there was a big collision on the motorway.
5. If one drives too quickly, you can cause an accident.
6. Educated at a good school and university, his suitability for a career with the firm was very apparent.
7. Standing on the terraces at the football match, my legs were aching badly.

Relevant Notes:
This type of **grammatical error** is common and is invariably caused by **carelessness** or **overambitious structure**, involving a confusion of clauses.

In scripts, **misrelated participles** are identified easily, because, as a general rule, the mismatch is between the

participle and the first word after the comma. This particular error is illustrated in the first three incorrect sentences earlier.

Explanations of the errors:
Sentence No. 1
'**Having told**' is a **verb form** called a **present participle**. The wording of the sentence must show clearly who did the telling. The structure of the sentence appears to suggest that '**it hasn't rained**' did the telling, which, of course, is ridiculous.

To produce a correct version, a little imagination is needed, in the absence of text to influence the wording.

Sentence No. 2
Here the **participle**, '**Thinking**', is misrelated to '**the UK**' and we have no way of knowing, from this text, who did the thinking.

In the absence of text, imagination is needed for the correction.

Sentence No. 3
'**Having said**' is totally unconnected in this very poorly written sentence with the consequence that the reader cannot determine who did the saying.

Once again imagination is needed to effect a correction in the absence of text.

Sentence No. 4
This sentence's fault is that it does not indicate who did the driving.

In the absence of guidance from the text, imagination is again exercised in the writing of a correct version.

Sentence No. 5
In this sentence there is a mismatch between '**one**' and '**you**'. The wording appears to suggest that, like '**one**', which is a **pronoun** in this context, and is used **impersonally**, the word '**you**' also is being used here **impersonally**, as it very often is, of course.

Although the two offending words mean the same in this usage, they are misrelated in that one version only of the **impersonal** usage would be more correct.

Better wording is, however, as follows: Driving too quickly can cause an accident.

Although the word '**Driving**' is a **present participle**, it is functioning as a **noun**, quite properly in this sentence.

Sentence No. 6
The mismatch is between '**educated**' and '**his suitability**'. This example shows that **misrelated participles** occur in both the **present** and **past** tenses.

Sentence No. 7
The mismatch is between '**Standing**' and '**my legs**'.

The revised versions of the sentences:
1. Having told you that the weather will be bad today, I got it wrong, because it hasn't rained at all yet and it's mid- afternoon now.
2. Thinking about the economic situation, I believe the UK must export more to help us to clear the deficit.
3. Having said that, I suggest, also, that the best thing we can do is stay here until it stops raining.
4. Last week, whilst I was driving home, there was a big collision on the motorway.
5. Driving too quickly can cause an accident.

6. Educated at a good school and university, he is suitable very apparently for a career with the firm.
7. When I was standing on the terraces at the football match, my legs were aching badly.

Now, go back to the original sentences and write them correctly without reference to these revised versions.

UNIT 10: CORRELATIVES

To be corrected:
1. I do not argue with neither my father or my mother.
2. Either we shall go to the cinema or we shall go to the theatre.
3. He was both deaf to criticism and to argument.
4. He was late, but not only that, he also came on the wrong day.
5. I hope to not just see my sister but my friend, Joan, next time I come here.
6. He not only decided what we ought to buy for lunch, but cooked it as well.
7. The policeman arrested the driver not just for being drunk but he was speaking on a mobile phone as well.
8. It is hardly right for us to be blamed for the damage if he caused it.
9. If he is joining us on the walk, he needs to get ready now.

Relevant Notes:
Correlatives are pairs of words, generally **conjunctions**, which are used in grammatical structures, although separately.
Conjunctions in sentences produce linkages, which will

be shown by means of the correction of the ten sentences.

Common mistakes that occur with the use of **correlatives** are: incorrect **pairings**, poor word order and incorrect choices of **pairings**.

Pairings
The most common are **co-ordinating correlatives** and less used ones are **subordinating correlatives**.

Co-ordinating correlatives include:
Both . . . and
Either . . . or
Neither . . . nor
Not only . . . but also.

Subordinating correlatives include:
Less . . . than
More . . . than
If . . . then
Hardly . . . when
So . . . that
Such . . . that

Explanations of the errors:
Sentence No. 1
Because the word **'not'** introduces the **negative** into the sentence, the use of **'neither'** which would then require **'nor'**, instead of **'either'**, would result in a **double negative**.

When correcting this sentence, we have a choice between: **'I do not argue with either my father or my mother'** and **'I argue with neither my father nor my mother.'**

Sentence No. 2
The word order is very poor, because **'we shall go'** is

featured twice, which is caused mainly by the **correlative pair** being too far apart.

Sentence No. 3
The word '**both**' can be moved closer to '**and**' to produce better wording as follows: '**He was deaf to both criticism and argument.**'

Sentence No. 4
The word order needs to be changed so that the **correlative** is **repaired** and positioned more properly in the script.

Sentence No. 5
The phrase '**not just**' may be used instead of '**not only**', but the change of '**but ... also**' to '**but ... as well**' is not advised. As with the previous sentence, the word order is not acceptable.

Sentence No. 6
The corrections required of the previous sentence need to be made for this sentence also.

Sentence No. 7
This sentence has the worst word order of the nine sentences and presents, consequently, an interesting challenge to the reader.
   Apart from a recommended change of '**as well**' to '**also**' the word choice is sound, but the arrangement of the words is extremely poor. In trying to produce a better and acceptable word order, the reader needs to position the **correlative pairing** much more closely.

Sentence No. 8
When the word '**if**' is used in this context, it means normally '**when**', which enables the use of the

correlative pairing. Generally, the alternative meaning of '**if**' questions whether **he did cause it**. The meaning intended would be apparent from how the word was said.

Sentence No. 9
The sentence, as it stands, is grammatically sound. The inclusion of the word '**then**' at the start of the clause after the comma is an improvement, however, and permits the full employment of the **subordinating correlative**.

The revised versions of the sentences:
1. I do not argue with either my father or my mother.
2. We shall go to either the cinema or the theatre.
3. He was deaf to both criticism and argument.
4. He was not only late, but also came on the wrong day.
5. Next time I come, I hope to see not only my sister, but also my friend, Joan.
6. He, not only decided what we ought to have, but also cooked it.
7. The policeman arrested the driver for not only being drunk, but also speaking on a mobile phone.
8. For us to be blamed for the damage is hardly right when he caused it.
9. If he is joining us on the walk, then he needs to get ready now.

Now, go back to the original sentences and write them correctly without reference to these revised versions.

UNIT 11: FUTURE TENSES

To be corrected:
1. I will try to get to work on time tomorrow.
2. I'm sorry to be shouting, but you <u>will</u> have to cut down on your smoking.
3. They shall be there very soon.
4. As your father, I'm telling you, for the last time, that, from now on, you, a child of ten years of age, <u>will</u> be home by eleven o'clock, at the latest.
5. At midday, I am waiting here for the past two hours.
6. According to the forecast, it is due to be raining in an hour's time.
7. They did not expect then, that they were going to have five children.
8. If he arrives at lunchtime, I have wasted a whole morning waiting for him to come.

Relevant Notes:
- Words that have been underlined above are to be emphasised.
- The **future** tense is mainly indicated by the use of either '**shall**' or '**will**', both of which tend to be used somewhat randomly. There is, however, a largely disregarded rule, which does govern their use.
- The rule is that, when used without emphasis, '**shall**'

is the correct choice for use with '**I**' and '**we**'. For use with '**he**', '**she**', '**you**', '**they**', or '**it**', when there is no emphasis, the correct word to use is '**will**'.
- When, however, there is emphasis, the opposite uses are correct. In short, when '**I**' is stressed, it is used with '**will**', and when '**you**' is stressed, it is used with '**shall**'.

Consider the following:
a) He is coming this afternoon.
b) The plane is landing at four o'clock tomorrow afternoon.
c) When the bell sounds, the lesson is over.
d) I am going on holiday tomorrow.

These sentences show how we use the **present** tense in a **future** context, which is a usage not confined to the English language.

Also, we have a **future perfect** tense. Examples are:
a) I shall have walked for an hour, when I get there.
b) The surgery will have closed for at least twenty minutes when I arrive.

A development upon this tense is the **future perfect continuous** tense, which would cause the above sentences to be adjusted to the following:
a) I shall have been walking for an hour, when I get there.
b) The surgery will have been closed for at least twenty minutes when I arrive.

Then, there is the **future in the past** tense. Examples are:
a) We were to be blamed for losing the dog on our walk.

b) He never suspected that they would become bitter rivals.

It is especially interesting to note the use of the word '**would**' in the last sentence. This word will appear again for fuller treatment in Unit 12.

Explanations of the errors:
Sentence No. 1
The word '**will**' is incorrect and needs to be changed to '**shall**', when not stressed and used with '**I**'.

Sentence No. 2
The word '**will**' is incorrect and needs to be changed to '**shall**', when stressed and used with '**you**'.

Sentence No. 3
The word '**shall**' is incorrect and needs to be changed to '**will**', when not stressed and used with '**they**'.

Sentence No. 4
The word '**will**' is incorrect and needs to be changed to '**shall**', when stressed and used with '**you**'.

Sentence No. 5
The error here is the use of '**am waiting**' for the **future perfect continuous** tense. The correction is '**shall have been**'. Also, the words '**the past**' can be deleted.

Sentence No. 6
There are three possible corrections to this sentence. The first is to change '**be raining**' to '**rain**', the second is to delete '**is due to be raining**' and insert '**will rain**'. The third one is to simply delete '**is due to**' and insert '**will**'.

Sentence No. 7
The structure of the sentence is acceptable grammatically without change, but an alternative, possibly improved, structure results from deleting '**were going to**' and inserting '**would**'.
 A reduction in word count is generally desirable, so long as the meaning is maintained.

Sentence No. 8
The word '**have**' needs to be changed to '**shall have**', which is the **future perfect** tense.

The revised versions of the sentences:
1. I shall try to get to work on time tomorrow.
2. I'm sorry to be shouting, but you shall have to cut down on your smoking.
3. They will be there very soon.
4. As your father, I'm telling you, for the last time, that, from now on, you, a child of ten years of age, shall be home by eleven o'clock, at the latest.
5. At midday, I shall have been waiting here for two hours.
6. According to the forecast, it will be raining in an hour's time.
7. They did not expect then, that they would have five children.
8. If he arrives at lunchtime, I shall have wasted a whole morning waiting for him to come.

Now, go back to the original sentences and write them correctly without reference to these revised versions.

UNIT 12: ACTIVE AND PASSIVE

To be changed:
1. My brother gave me a watch for my birthday.
2. The new dress was worn by my aunt.
3. The farmer drove his tractor very dangerously.
4. You believed it would rain this afternoon.
5. A broken teapot was thrown into the rubbish bin by Alice.
6. Mary said she would be here by lunchtime.
7. A large log was put on the fire by my father.
8. The new car was bought by him.
9. We do not accept the claim for damages.
10. Too much money was wasted by us on useless Christmas presents last year.

Relevant Notes:
- In the above list, some of the sentences are written in the **active voice**, and the others are in the **passive voice**.
- In a sentence written in the **active voice**, the **subject performs the action**, or **causes whatever process or event** is described by the verb.
- Whereas, in a sentence written in the **passive voice**, the **subject** is the recipient of the action which is described by the verb.

Consider: The dog chased the rabbit.
'**The dog**' is the **subject**; '**chased**' is the verb; '**the rabbit**' is the **object**.
The sentence is in the *active* **voice**.

Consider, now, a sentence, written in the *passive* **voice**: The rabbit is chased by the dog.
The two sentences report the same occurrence, despite the differences in their wording.

The **active voice** is more used than the **passive voice**, but to maintain a reader's interest in a script, such as an essay, the writer is advised to try to use both of the **voices**.

In speech, the **passive voice** is used even less by most people and yet, again, varying between the **voices** does afford the speaker variety in his or her command of language.

Study the sentences at the beginning of Unit 12 and decide which are written in the active and which in the passive. Then check your decisions with the following and reword the sentences to change the voice of each, as required:

Sentence No. 1
Active is to be changed to **passive**.

Sentence No. 2
Passive is to be changed to **active**.

Sentence No. 3
Active is to be changed to **passive**.

Sentence No. 4
Active is to be changed to **passive**.

Sentence No. 5
Passive is to be changed to **active**.

Sentence No. 6
Active is to be changed to **passive**.

Sentence No. 7
Passive is to be changed to **active**.

Sentence No. 8
Passive is to be changed to **active**.

Sentence No. 9
Active is to be changed to **passive**.

Sentence No. 10
Passive is to be changed to **active**.

The changed versions of the sentences:
1. I was given a watch by my brother for my birthday.
2. My aunt wore the new dress.
3. The tractor was driven very dangerously by the farmer.
4. It was believed by you that it would rain this afternoon.
5. Alice threw a broken teapot into the rubbish bin.
6. It was said by Mary that she would be here by lunchtime.
7. My father put a large log on the fire.
8. He bought the new car.
9. The claim for damages is not accepted by us.
10. We wasted too much money on useless Christmas presents last year.

Now, go back to the original sentences and write them down in the changed versions from active to passive voice, or from passive to active voice, as applicable.

UNIT 13: OUGHT/SHOULD/WOULD CONDITIONAL TENSE AND CLAUSE

To be corrected:
1. You hadn't ought to do it.
2. I should like to welcome you to this meeting and to thank you for coming.
3. I hope you are not suggesting that I did anything I didn't ought.
4. You should of said that you were coming.
5. I said you will find out in the end.
6. If I could climb that tree, I would be able to rescue the cat stuck up there.
7. If it is sunny tomorrow, we can go on the beach.

Relevant Notes:
- The words **'would'** and **'should'** are **modal auxiliary verbs**, as are: **'may'**, **'might'**, **'can'**, **'could'**, **'will'**, **'shall'** and **'must'** – which are sometimes known as more simply **modals** or **auxiliaries**.

  They have to precede main verbs, although, sometimes, they are isolated in speech and script. When, however, this happens, the main verb is implied.

The word **'should'** may be used instead of **'ought to'**, as follows: I ought to go to see the doctor this morning. I should go to see the doctor this morning.

In this context, the other **subject pronouns** can be used also. So, for instance, it would be correct to write or say: You ought to go to see the doctor. You should go to see the doctor.

Both of these sentences infer **obligation** in contrast to the following in which the words '**ought**' and '**should**' can infer either **expectation** or **obligation**: She ought to telephone shortly. She should telephone shortly.

If either of these sentences were spoken in such a way as to suggest that she were likely to telephone shortly, there would be **expectation**. Were the sentence written, however, it would not be apparent whether **expectation** or **obligation** applied.

The word '**should**' is used also before verbs of **liking**, **thinking**, **saying**, **caring**, **imagining** and **preferring**.

Also, it is used in verbal structures such as: **I should be glad** and **I should be inclined**.

The words '**should**' and '**would**' can be used, also, in the context of expressing the **future in the past**, an example of which is as follows: When we met twenty years ago, we never suspected that we should become friends for life.

Technically, it is accepted generally, that '**should**' is used with '**I**' and '**we**' and that '**would**' is used in conjunction with all the other **subject pronouns**, but this technicality is no longer respected, other than by purists.

More commonly the words '**should**' and '**would**' have become virtually interchangeable despite which it is recommended that the technicality be respected, meaning that '**should**' be used with '**I**' and '**we**' and '**would**' be used for the other **subject pronouns**, as stated above. Obviously, this ruling does not apply when '**should**' is used as an alternative to '**ought**', and instead of '**if**' and '**unless**' in connection with the **conditional** tense, yet to be explained.

'**Should**' and '**would**' are used also in the **subjunctive mood**, which is addressed in the next unit.

Conditional Tense
Consider the following sentences:
- If you could climb that tree, you would be able to rescue the cat stuck up there.
- If you were able to climb that tree, you could rescue the cat stuck up there.
- Were you able to climb that tree, you could rescue the cat stuck up there.

All the above sentences are perfectly sound, grammatically, and illustrate **condition**.

Consider, now, the two forms of **condition** illustrated by the following:
- We shall be working in the garden this afternoon, if it doesn't rain.
- Unless you tell me differently, I shall assume we are staying at home this evening.

Both sentences feature **conditional clauses**, being '**if it doesn't rain**' and '**unless you tell me differently**'.

What is especially interesting is that both sentences are produced in the **present** tense – perfectly correctly – despite referring to the future.

The word '**if**' is the most common starting word to a **conditional clause**, and it is interesting to see that the word '**unless**' has the same grammatical effect here.

Alternative wording for the two sentences incorporates another use of the word '**should**' as follows:
- Should it not rain, we shall be working in the garden this afternoon.

- Should you not tell me differently, I shall assume we are staying at home this evening.

Clause

Although you will have become familiar, by now, with **sentence structures**, you have encountered the word **clause** for the first time and, therefore, an explanation of the term is called for.

Consider the sentence: When I lived in France, I was very young.

This sentence features two **clauses**, being:
- When I lived in France,
- I was very young.

The first is called a **subordinate clause**, and the second is a **main clause**.

Had the positions of the two **clauses** been reversed in the sentence, this would not have changed their functions as **main** or **subordinate clauses**.

You will note that the **main clause** could stand alone as a sentence, not needing the support of the **subordinate clause** to form a proper sentence. Invariably, but not always, **main clauses** can stand alone in this way and be perfectly sound sentences in their own right.

Moreover, there can be more than one **main clause** in a sentence and not all sentences feature a **subordinate clause**. On the other hand, there can be several **subordinate clauses** in a sentence and there are several types of such **clauses**.

The word '**subordinate**' means that such a clause has lesser importance to the extent that it cannot function as a sentence in its own right. In short, a **subordinate clause** is merely a development upon a **main clause**.

As already mentioned, there are several types of **subordinate clauses**, which the reader may decide to investigate, in conjunction with a more developed understanding of the subject of **clauses** in general, but for the purposes of this study no such development is considered essential.

Explanations of the errors:
Sentence No. 1
The use of '**hadn't ought**' is a fairly common mistake and is especially odd usage when it is considered that the sentence is in the **present** tense.

Sentence No. 2
Technically, the wording is perfectly acceptable, as a particular note before shows, but the expression is over-wordy and is too commonly used for it to be a good way to start a speech at, for instance, a wedding reception.

Sentence No. 3
'**I didn't ought**' is fairly common as also is '**I didn't ought to have done**'. Both are clumsy wording and need to be replaced by '**I shouldn't have done**'.

Sentence No. 4
The word '**of**' here, like '**of**' featured in Unit 4, Sentence No. 7, is a far too common error in both speech and script.

Sentence No. 5
The word '**will**' is the wrong choice here. What is required is the word to register **the future in the past**.

Sentence No. 6
'**Would**' is the offending word here.

Sentence No. 7
Although the use of the **present** tense for the whole

sentence is acceptable, it is better to use the **future** tense of the verb '**to be able**' after the comma in this instance

The revised versions of the sentences:
1. You ought not to do it.
2. Welcome and thank you for coming.
3. I hope you are not suggesting that I did anything that I should not have done.
4. You ought to have said that you were coming.
5. I said you would find out in the end.
6. If I could climb that tree, I should be able to rescue the cat stuck up there.
7. If it is sunny tomorrow, we shall be able to go on the beach.

In Sentence No. 1, however, '**ought not to**' may be supplanted by '**should not**' and in Sentence No. 4 '**should**' may be used instead of '**ought to**'.

Now, go back to the original sentences and write them correctly without reference to these revised versions.

UNIT 14: THE SUBJUNCTIVE

To be corrected:
1. If I was you, I'd not work so hard.
2. It is absolutely vital that you are there this evening.
3. We insist that he appears in public to explain his conduct.
4. He demanded that we were there by two o'clock this afternoon.
5. If he was here, I'd tell him what I think about his unreliability.
6. He talked as if what he said was the answer to all our problems.
7. If she was to win the lottery, will she buy a new car?
8. If he was my husband, he would have to get a job.
9. We'd go for a walk, if it wasn't raining.
10. I suggested he should write to apologise.

Relevant Notes:
- This unit is likely to prove to be the most challenging one in the pack for the student who is encountering the **subjunctive** for the first time.

The Three Moods

Consider:
- The **indicative mood**, sometimes known as the **declarative mood**, features the grammatical mood of the verb that makes a statement, i.e. a declaration, which means it features **declarative** verbs, or poses a question, which means it also features **interrogative** verbs.
- The **imperative mood** features the grammatical mood of the verb that produces an **order/command** with the sentence sometimes, but not always, ending with an exclamation mark in script.
- The **subjunctive mood** is used when there is a hypothetical connection between the subject of the sentence and the predicate or between the two clauses, i.e. the main and subordinate clauses.

All the sentences in the units of the pack to date are in the **indicative mood**.

The following sentences are examples of the **imperative mood**:
a) Go to the shop and buy a bottle of milk.
b) Don't come here tomorrow, because I'm going out.
c) Stop!

The **subjunctive mood** has **three** versions, as follows:
- The **formulaic**, or **optative**, **subjunctive**, which is used to communicate a wish/desire of which examples are: God bless you, Long live the queen and So be it.
- The **mandative subjunctive**, which is used when a command is inferred, although the wording is not in

the **imperative**. So, an example is: I insist you be there this evening. Another one is: The manager has demanded that he finish the job by lunchtime.

- The **past subjunctive** is the most likely structure to be recognised, because it reveals in the use of '**were**'. So, an example is: If I were you, I should try to lose weight. Another one is: Try to imagine the outcome, if he were to leave the business.

Of these, the **formulaic subjunctive** is not worth too much discussion, because the uses of it are limited.

In the first example of a **mandative subjunctive** given above, perhaps the wording **I insist you *are* there** might have been more familiar, but that would have been in the **indicative mood** and, therefore, incorrect. It is important to note that whatever person, singular or plural, is fitted into that sentence – **he, she, it, we, you** or **they** – the verb is still '**be**'.

Similarly, in the second sentence, it would have still been '**finish**' whatever the **subject** or **subject pronoun**, singular or plural.

In the other two examples, both relating to the **past** tense of the **subjunctive mood**, the verb '**were**' would have been correct, regardless of the **subject person**. Interestingly, the habitual use of the word '**were**' has resulted in the **past subjunctive** sometimes being described as the **were-subjunctive**.

The other complication with the use of the **subjunctive** is the use of the **conditional** tense i.e. '**should**' and '**would**', which it entails.

In Unit 13, the uses of '**would**' and '**should**' were highlighted and are now increased by their use in the **subjunctive**.

Words that are incorrect and need to be changed into the subjunctive mood:
Sentence No. 1
The use of '**was**' is incorrect.

Sentence No. 2
The use of '**are**' is incorrect.

Sentence No. 3
The use of '**appears**' is incorrect.

Sentence No. 4
The use of '**were**' is incorrect.

Sentence No. 5
The use of '**was**' is incorrect.

Sentence No. 6
The use of '**was**' is incorrect.

Sentence No. 7
The use of '**was**' and '**will**' is incorrect.

Sentence No. 8
The use of '**was**' is incorrect.

Sentence No. 9
The use of '**we'd**' is poor and '**wasn't**' is incorrect.

Sentence No. 10
The use of '**should**' is incorrect.

The revised versions of the sentences:
1. If I were you, I should not work so hard.
2. It is absolutely vital that you be there this evening.
3. We insist that he appear in public to explain his conduct.
4. He demanded that we be there by two o'clock this afternoon.
5. If he were here, I should tell him what I think about his unreliability.
6. He talked as if what he said were the answer to all our problems.
7. If she were to win the lottery, would she buy a new car?
8. If he were my husband, he would have to get a job.
9. We should go for a walk, if it were not raining.
10. I suggested that he write to apologise.

It should be noted that, whilst '**I should**' and '**We should**' are featured in the revised sentences, '**I'd**' and '**We'd**' are acceptable also, being satisfactory, shortened versions of '**I should**' and '**We should**'.

Now, go back to the original sentences and write them correctly without reference to these revised versions.

UNIT 15: SPOT THE GAFF!

To be corrected:
1. I was so fascinated by the film that my eyes were literally glued to the screen from start to finish.
2. There was no play at Lord's today, in spite of it being fine.
3. I think he is in his 50's.
4. There will be a bit of rain in Wales tomorrow.
5. We shall be home by 12 p.m. at the latest.
6. The data in the record was false.
7. So, therefore, we cannot attend your party tonight.
8. I only wanted to watch the game on television.
9. At the end of the day, I shall do my best to score in the match this afternoon.
10. Well, you know, at this moment in time he's thinking of changing his job.
11. I was decimated when I learned about your accident.
12. It is definitely going to rain this afternoon.
13. He is disinterested in politics, so he will not vote in the election.
14. My older brother is my best friend.
15. There are less people in church today.
16. Me and Robert are going to the match this afternoon.
17. It's me.
18. I, myself, don't think like that.

19. I, personally, don't agree with what you are saying.
20. I've found out that it was him who paid for the lunch.

Relevant Notes:
The sentences exhibit a mix of poor **common usage** featuring a mix of **errors, nonsense** and **verbosity**, in spoken or written English, which explains the use of the word '**Gaff**' in the heading.

The claim made that they are *common* mistakes will become apparent to the reader, who, having been made aware of them, will spot them and be surprised how often they occur in normal conversation or script, as applicable, even by people who should know better.

Explanations of the gaffs:
Sentence No. 1
The offending word is '**literally**', which means '**truly**' or '**exactly**'. Thus, we are exposed to the horrendous impression of eyes being stuck on a screen.

Sentence No. 2
The phrase '**it being**' is the problem here and, although this structure is common, it is not grammatically correct; '**its being**' is correct, but '**although the weather was fine**' is better.

Sentence No. 3
The apostrophe is perhaps the most misused punctuation mark and yet its uses are comparatively few. Here, it should not be used at all.

Sentence No. 4
On television, weather forecasters warn us that we can expect a bit of rain, seemingly ignorant of the fact that there cannot be a bit of a substance that cannot be split into bits.

Sentence No. 5
There are no such times as **12 p.m.** and **12 a.m.** The correct versions of these times are: **12 midnight**, and **12 midday**, or **noon**.

Sentence No. 6
To be '**Data**', information should not be false.

Sentence No. 7
One of the meanings of '**so**' is '**therefore**'. Consequently, either '**so**' or '**therefore**' is redundant in the sentence. A similar mistake is the usage of a pairing from '**also**', '**as well**' and '**too**' in the same sentence. An example of duplication is as follows: **We, also, will be there, as well.**

Sentence No. 8
The word '**only**' can cause misunderstanding if it is misplaced in a sentence, or punctuation is absent or careless.

a)   I, only, wanted to watch the game on television.
b)   I wanted to watch the game, only, on television.
c)   I wanted, only, to watch the game on television.

- The meaning of the first sentence is: **I, alone, wanted to watch the game on television.**
- The meaning of the second sentence is: **I didn't want to watch anything on television except the game.**
- The meaning of the third sentence is: **I didn't want to do anything other than watch the game on the television.**

The position of the comma is critical to the meaning of the sentence.
   Normally, in the case of a sentence of this complexity being spoken, appropriate emphasis manages to convey

the intended meaning, even when the word '**only**' is misplaced.

Sentence No. 9
The use of the tiresome expression '**at the end of the day**' here is pointless and, indeed, causes the wording of the sentence overall to be ridiculous. Such expressions have no validity in language and their imitation should be resisted.

Sentence No. 10
This sentence is littered with faults.

'**Well**' is used here as the opening word to a spoken reply and is used very commonly as a short delay to permit the speaker to formulate his or her response to the question posed. So long as it is used sparingly it is acceptable, but some people overuse it and it is then in the same category as '**you know**' which is a stopgap and is as unnecessary as '**at the end of the day**'.

Some people develop the unfortunate habit of using such expressions without realising, presumably, how adversely their language is affected as a consequence.

'**At this precise moment of time**' is probably the silliest phrase in the twenty sentences of this unit, because, although the word '**moment**' has also the meaning of '**importance**', it cannot mean anything but a '**moment of time**' in the text, so '**of time**' is unnecessary wording. Moreover, the word '**precise**' is not needed simply because the wording '**at this moment**' is precise. Then, the idea that one can know what another person is thinking at a precise moment is clearly ridiculous.

Sentence No. 11
To decimate means to destroy or kill a large number of people and originates from Roman times when a tenth

of captured men would be killed by the army if they mutinied. Clearly, this verb is an inappropriate choice here and '**shocked**' would be a better choice.

Sentence No. 12
The word '**definitely**' is an unsuitable choice here, because its correct use is limited to an expression of absolute certainty and even the professional weather forecasters cannot produce totally reliable forecasts.

Sentence No. 13
The word '**disinterested**' is incorrect here, because it means '**free from bias or partiality**'. The correct word is '**uninterested**'. This error is curious in that of the two words '**disinterested**' is used the more commonly, despite being incorrect.

Sentence No. 14
The use of the word '**older**' is incorrect in this sentence, as the following correct sentences illustrate:
- I know several people who are fitter than I despite being much older.
- Old people at the show included my elder brother and his best friend, Albert.
- I have three brothers and the oldest is the fittest of the four of us.
- The oldest member of the family is treated with special respect because he, or she, is the eldest.

Note that the word '**oldest**' is the **superlative** of the word '**old**', and is, therefore, an **adjective**, which means that it is a **describing** word.
The word '**eldest**' is a noun, meaning the **oldest** person. Note, however, that the word '**elder**' can be either an adjective or a noun. As an **adjective**, like '**older**', it is

the **comparative** form of the word '**old**'. As a noun an elder can be an elder of a church or chapel.

Sentence No 15
The use of '**less**' when '**fewer**' is required is another very common error. Consider the following correct sentences:
- There is less need for me to get up early in the morning.
- I am less able to write a good letter than you are.
- These days I meet fewer of my old friends when I'm in town.
- There are fewer people in church today.

Sentence No. 16
This type of error is common and is one of the most inexcusable mistakes, because anyone saying it would be very unlikely to make the mistake of saying, '**Me am going**'.

Sentence No. 17
This error is even more common than the previous one and is of the same type in that it features '**me**' being used instead of '**I**'.

It is different, however, in that its correct version is seldom used, which, perhaps, would seem to make the error excusable.

Sentence No. 18
The word '**myself**', although perfectly correct, grammatically, is not required unless it is being used as an **intensifier**, to produce emphasis.

Sentence No. 19
The word '**personally**', like '**myself**' in the previous sentence, is unnecessary, but, again, it may be used for emphasis, which would be acceptable.

Sentence No. 20
The error in this sentence is the use of '**him**', which should be '**he**' – being the **subject**, not the **object**, of the verb '**was**'.

This mistake is similar to the errors in previous sentences (16 and 17), in which the common failing is the lack of recognition of what is the true **subject** of the verb.

The revised versions of the sentences:
1. I was so fascinated by the film that I couldn't take my eyes off the screen from start to finish.
2. There was no play at Lord's today, although it was fine.
3. I think he is in his 50s.
4. There will be light rain in Wales tomorrow.
5. We shall be home by 12 midnight at the latest.
6. The information in the record was false.
7. Therefore, we cannot attend your party tonight.
8. I wanted only to watch the game on television.
9. I shall do my best to score in the match this afternoon.
10. Well, I understand that he is thinking of changing his job.
11. I was shocked when I learned about your accident.
12. I believe it is going to rain this afternoon.
13. He is uninterested in politics, so he will not vote in the election.
14. My elder brother is my best friend.
15. There are fewer people in church today.
16. Robert and I are going to the match this afternoon.
17. It is I.
18. I don't think like that.
19. I don't agree with what you are saying.
20. I've found out that it was he who paid for the lunch.

Now, go back to the original sentences and write them correctly without reference to these revised versions.

FINALLY!

Test yourself by correcting the following:
1. My horse is running quicker than yours, but neither of us are going to be collecting winnings for this race.
2. I am the least fortunate of the two of us.
3. Of the two goalkeepers, he's the best in my opinion.
4. It doesn't matter whom you are, it's to do with how reliable you are, I believe.
5. He might do very well in the future.
6. Can you help me with my homework tomorrow?
7. Everybody likes to enjoy themselves on New Year's Eve.
8. He doesn't know nothing about sport.
9. None of you are good enough to get into the first team.
10. Me and Arthur finished the job by lunchtime.
11. All the family is taking exercise to get fit.
12. Having said that, the weather will change this evening.
13. It's not just wearing nice clothes to look good, you have to keep your hands out of your pockets as well.
14. You shall have to do better in the examination next week.
15. I would prefer to decide tomorrow, whether I'm going to the party.

Corrected versions:
1. My horse is running more quickly than yours, but neither of us is going to be collecting winnings for this race.
2. I am the less fortunate of the two of us.
3. Of the two goalkeepers, he's the better in my opinion.
4. It doesn't matter who you are, it's to do with how reliable you are, I believe.
5. He may do very well in the future.
6. Will you be able to help me with my homework tomorrow?
7. All people like to enjoy themselves on New Year's Eve.
8. He knows nothing about sport.
9. None of you is good enough to get into the first team.
10. Arthur and I finished the job by lunchtime.
11. All the family are taking exercise to get fit.
12. Having said that, I think the weather will change this evening.
13. To look good, it's not only wearing nice clothes, but also keeping your hands out of your pockets.
14. You will have to do better in the examination next week.
15. I should prefer to decide tomorrow, whether or not I shall be going to the party.

Congratulations!

You've finished the course and, hopefully, it has proved to be, as promised at the outset, an *easier way* to improve your spoken and written English language.

PUNCTUATION

AN EASIER WAY

This self-study pack is intended to provide *an easier way* by which the student can achieve reasonable proficiency in the use of the main punctuation marks.

Each of the marks selected for study is the main feature of a unit, in the pack of 15 units, with its function(s) being illustrated by means of a number of sentences and explained by short, simply worded notes.

Subsequent to having received this individual attention, the mark is then included in sentences featured in units that follow to permit progressive reinforcement of its usage.

On completion of the units, the student is invited to attempt to correct misuse, or absence, of punctuation marks in twenty sentences.

It is expected that the student will become markedly more competent in the use of the punctuation marks featured and will be, consequently, more comfortable and confident in the event of having to sit examinations requiring the writing of scripts in the English language.

UNIT 1: THE FULL STOP (.)

Examples of usage:
1. My name is John.
2. I am English and live in Bristol.
3. My birthday is in the month of April.
4. I have a friend who lives in the Yorkshire Dales.
5. I think Queen Elizabeth is a wonderful lady.
6. Most children in Britain enjoy Christmas more than any other time of the year.
7. Every August Bank Holiday I make a visit to North Wales.
8. My wife and I spend as much time as we can in France.
9. Capitalisation is the use of the **upper case** and is featured in several of the sentences in Unit 1.
10. I have finished reading *Bruno's Dream* by Iris Murdoch and recommend it to you.

Notes:
- The full stop is a **terminator**.
- This means that its use signals the end of an **utterance**.
- A characteristic of all sentences is that the first letter of the first word is a **capital letter**.
- **Capitalisation** is a feature of several of the ten sentences above and of sentences in other units to come to enable the reader to become aware of when capitals are needed.

UNIT 2: THE QUESTION MARK (?)

Examples of usage:
1. Why are you late for work?
2. Did you have any breakfast this morning?
3. What is your name?
4. Do you like to swim?
5. How old are you?
6. Have you ever been to Manchester?
7. Do you agree that smoking is bad for your health?
8. Are they friends of yours?
9. Shall we meet on Thursday?
10. Should we speak to him about his unreliability?

Notes:
- The question mark is a **terminator**.
- The mark itself features a full stop and is a useful reminder that it does terminate an **utterance**. It does not have quite the same value, however, as the full stop, which will be explained in Unit 15.
- Notice that all the first words of the sentences above start with a **capital letter**.
- The sentences in both units so far (1 and 2) are **statements**.
- The difference between these two types of statement is that the ones in Unit 1 are called **declarative sentences** and the ones in Unit 2 are **interrogative sentences**.

UNIT 3: THE COMMA (,)

Examples of usage:
1. Sometimes, I have seen a woodpecker in this wood.
2. You need, however, to be careful when you cross this busy road.
3. I bought apples, pears, plums and oranges at this stall.
4. Mary James, the best teacher this school ever had, retired last year.
5. Will you help me, please?
6. If I remember correctly, today is your birthday.
7. Actually, I did not go to the theatre last evening, but stayed at home watching television.
8. I enjoy playing all sports, particularly soccer, cricket, rugby and tennis.
9. Smiling happily, he went forward to receive the first prize in the raffle.
10. My uncle, who is an architect, designed the frontage of the new office building.

Notes:
- The comma is a **separator**, as shown by the examples above, where it causes separation of parts of the sentences.
- When we speak, we tend to punctuate our speech

automatically by raising or lowering our voices and by making pauses of varying lengths. For this reason, when punctuating script, it makes sense to read aloud what we have written and be guided by how we speak, especially if we have problems with punctuation.

- Short pauses, generally without significant raising or lowering of the voice, call for **separators** in script.
- There is, however, a recognised tendency for the comma to be overused with the result that unnecessary pauses can be induced in the reading.

UNIT 4: THE EXCLAMATION MARK (!)

Examples of usage:
1. Give it to me!
2. Wow!
3. Good heavens!
4. Congratulations!
5. How disgusting!
6. Behave yourself!
7. Well done!
8. Imagine doing that!
9. Brilliant!
10. Help me, please!

Notes:
- The exclamation mark is a **terminator** and, like the question mark, the mark itself does include a full stop, which does not have entirely the same value as the full stop discussed in Unit 1 as will be explained in Unit 15.
- An exclamation is an **utterance**, even when it features one word only, as is the case with several examples above.
- Not all exclamations need to end with an exclamation mark, illustrated by the following sentence: **What a shame that he wasn't able to be here.**

- Exclamations of several words tend not to need the mark, mainly because they lack suddenness of the likes of the examples to register **surprise** or **shock** or **give an order**, in **imperative mood**.
- Often, exclamations are delivered loudly and are involuntary reactions.
- As with the use of the comma, there is a tendency for the exclamation mark to be overused, but it is essential that the question mark be used always when a question is being asked.
- Statements that are commands are **imperative sentences**, and those that are exclamations are **exclamatory sentences**.

UNIT 5: THE COLON (:)

Examples of usage:
1. The man was big and powerful: he was really threatening.
2. There was no point in his staying with the firm any longer: he hadn't got the promotion he expected.
3. When you are packing to go on holiday be sure to include: changes of clothing, toiletries, extra shoes and sandals, underwear, travel guides and documents, euros, credit and debit cards, and cash, as necessary.
4. If you want to learn a foreign language well, I suggest that you:
   - Listen to audio tapes.
   - Study a recommended book of grammar.
   - Enrol for a course at college, if there is one.
   - Practise the language orally at any opportunity.
   - Take your holidays in the country where the language is spoken.

Notes:
- The colon is a **separator**.
- In sentences 1 and 2, the colon is used, because in each of them, there is a direct linkage between the two clauses to the extent that they constitute '**cause and effect**'. Each clause could stand alone as a sentence in

its own right, as each is a **main clause**.
- A clause is a group of words, generally including a **subject** and a verb, and there are three types of clause, being a **main clause**, a **subordinate clause** and a **non-finite clause**.
- Whilst **subordinate clauses** and **non-finite clauses** cannot stand alone, a **main clause** can.

Example of a **main clause**: they cheered loudly.
Example of a **subordinate clause**: when he scored a goal.
Example of a **non-finite clause**: playing in his first game.

Notes:
- '**They**' is the **subject** and '**cheered**' the verb in the **main clause**.
- The conjunction '**when**' introduces the **subordinate clause**.
- '**Playing**' is not a finite verb, resulting in the **non-finite clause**.

All three clauses can be merged into a sentence: They cheered loudly, when, playing in his first game, he scored a goal.

UNIT 6: THE APOSTROPHE (')

Examples of usage:
1. Let's go for a walk in the park.
2. It's possible, but not likely, that we shall see a woodpecker in this wood.
3. Who's the champion player at darts?
4. Isn't it a nice morning?
5. Aren't you able to help me?
6. We're trying to clean the cooker.
7. I shan't be there before noon.
8. I can't leave the house this morning.
9. There's somebody ringing the bell.
10. They've decided to buy a new car.

In all the above sentences the apostrophe is used to indicate that parts of words have been missed out.

Consider, now, the same sentences without the apostrophes:
1. Let us go for a walk in the park.
2. It is possible, but not likely, that we shall see a woodpecker in this wood.
3. Who is the champion player at darts?
4. Is it not a nice morning?
5. Are you not able to help me?
6. We are trying to clean the cooker.

7. I shall not be there before noon.
8. I cannot leave the house this morning.
9. There is somebody ringing the bell.
10. They have decided to buy a new car.

Examples of usage to indicate possession:
1. Fred's wife is much younger than he.
2. The baby's toys littered the floor.
3. The babies' toys littered the floor.
4. The boy's favourite sport is rugby.
5. The boys' favourite sport is rugby.
6. The men's department is on the first floor.
7. Mr Jones's shop is closed this morning.
8. Linda's failure to qualify disappointed us all.
9. Who is the people's choice?
10. The books' covers are very glossy.

Consider, now, the following, which are the same sentences minus the apostrophes:
1. The wife of Fred is much younger than he.
2. The toys of the baby littered the floor.
3. The toys of the babies littered the floor.
4. The favourite sport of the boy is rugby.
5. The favourite sport of the boys is rugby.
6. The department for men is on the first floor.
7. The shop of Mr Jones is closed this morning.
8. The failure by Linda to qualify disappointed us all.
9. Who is the choice of the people?
10. The covers of the books are very glossy.

Although the original sentences for both expressed '**possession**' it should be noted that sentences 6 and 8 include '**for**' and '**by**', respectively, as more appropriate prepositions than '**of**', when the apostrophes are removed.

Examples of usage relating to time and dates:
1. I expect to be there in an hour's time.
2. We shall try to be with you in two days' time.
3. It is nearly ten o'clock.
4. I was there in '95.

Exceptions:
The following examples show that there are exceptions to the rules relating to the use of the apostrophe:
- **My sisters-in-law's pony**, meaning, **the pony of my sisters-in-law**.
- **My sisters-in-law's ponies**, meaning, **the ponies of my sisters-in-law**.
- **Jesus' apostles**, meaning, **the apostles of Jesus**.
- **Achilles' heel**, meaning, **the heel of Achilles**.

Notes:
- The apostrophe is a **separator**.
- There are examples of words which although abbreviations of original words, have now become accepted as proper words in their reduced forms – examples are: **flu, photo** and **pram**.
- There are many shop signs and letter headings that do not include apostrophes in the business names, despite the fact that such names are corruptions without the correct punctuation.

REVISION

To enable reinforcement of the correct use of the punctuation marks introduced to this stage in the pack, consider the following with care:
1. He was tall, if I remember correctly, and had broad shoulders.
2. She was absolutely beautiful!
3. When it is time to leave, I shall let you know.
4. If you don't listen to what you are told in class, you won't learn.
5. He was a pleasant, smart, cheerful and friendly teenager.
6. Are you coming to see me this afternoon?
7. Why are you so unhappy?
8. I'll meet you outside Marks & Spencer at ten o'clock.
9. I bought my first motorbike in the '70s.
10. He was extremely disappointed to see that the snails had eaten his lettuce: he'll never try to grow anything but flowers in future.

UNIT 7: THE SEMICOLON (;)

Examples of usage:
1. I've had my breakfast; I've been shopping; I've done the housework; now, I'm preparing the lunch.
2. We arrived home late; we had a bit of supper; we went to bed.
3. When you have an essay to write, you should prepare properly before committing pen to paper by:
   - Researching the topic thoroughly;
   - Making sure that the results of the research will satisfy the demands of the essay;
   - Producing the essay plan;
   - Writing the essay in rough form;
   - Checking the grammar, spelling and punctuation;
   - Rewriting the essay with care to ensure it is progressed properly with appropriate linkages;
   - Checking the word count is in keeping with the stipulated length in the brief;
   - Getting it read by someone whose opinion you value as being forthright and constructive.

Notes:
- The semicolon is a **separator**.
- It is used to link clauses that are similar in meaning, but could be used as individual sentences.

- It is used in listings, such as in the third sentence, when it is an alternative to full stops.
- It can be used instead of conjunctions, such as '**then**', as shown in the second sentence.

UNIT 8: THE HYPHEN (-)

Examples of usage:
1. My mother-in-law is coming to tea today.
2. If you enjoy nail-biting suspense, you must watch the film on television this evening.
3. My father is eighty-four years of age next Wednesday.
4. I had to go to the hospital for an X-ray this morning.
5. In less than a year there has been a two-fold increase in the cost of petrol at our local filling station.
6. I was taking a walk in the Shropshire countryside, when a passer-by asked me for directions to Church Stretton.
7. My brother and I are both hard-working people, because our father was a self-made man.

Notes:
- The hyphen is a **separator**.
- Its most common use is to form compound words by joining two or more words to produce a hyphenated word, such as **tax-free** or **crash-land**.
- The words can be nouns, such as **brother** and **law**, to produce **brother-in-law**, or a prefix and a noun, such as **post-** and **war** to produce **post-war**, or a

prefix and a verb, such as **re-** and **advertise**, to produce **re-advertise**.
- Apart from the examples given, there are other compounds which are a common feature of the English language involving a variety of combinations, mostly in the form of **noun compounds**.
- In the example sentences, '**X-ray**' is shown as an example of a **noun compound** resulting from the joining by a hyphen of a letter and a noun. This type of combination is fairly common and further examples of it are: **G-string** and **T-bone**.

UNIT 9: THE ELLIPSIS (. . .)

Examples of usage:
1. He wrote to me and accused me of being a selfish, arrogant . . . I have replied and, obviously, I resisted the temptation to be as rude as he was.
2. There are many forms of bad behaviour, like swearing, littering the streets, treating others with disrespect . . . so it's a nice change to see that there are exceptions in society.
3. One day, perhaps, I shall manage to grow potatoes, cabbages, carrots . . . that I shall be able to enter in the gardening competition.
4. The property was a disaster with old bits of furniture, newspaper cuttings, broken glass, bird droppings . . . showing how long it had been forsaken.
5. Next time you visit us, we shall be able to go into town, have a meal, watch a football match . . . whatever you fancy doing.

Notes:
- The ellipsis is used as either a **terminator** or a **separator**, because it can be used at any point in a script.
- The ellipsis is used to indicate the omission of text

without providing an indication of how many words are missing.
- Three full stops are used regardless of the number of words missing from the script, although, exceptionally, a whole line of stops is sometimes used to signify the omission of a complete line, or even a stanza.
- Like the question mark and the exclamation mark, the ellipsis features the full stop appropriate to its function as a **terminator**, but, of course, this characteristic is not always clear, firstly, because of the use of three stops, not one, and, secondly, because of its other function as a **separator**.
- The plural of ellipsis is **ellipses**.

UNIT 10: THE DASH (–)

Examples of usage:
1. Tomorrow – weather permitting – we shall take a trip to the coast.
2. His disinclination to get involved – although he would stand to benefit if what we are planning does succeed – is not really fair.
3. She was the most astute member of the group – invariably the quickest to foresee any problems – and generally the one to produce a solution.
4. When I think things could go badly – not everyone is as sensitive as I am to warning signs – they often do.
5. We met for the first time last year – a memorable occasion on the coast at Barmouth – and now we are going to get married.

Notes:
- The dash is a **separator**.
- Dashes are an alternative to brackets, as also to commas, when they are used as parentheses, as they are in all the sentences above.
- Although the dash does not usually have its own key on the computer keyboard, there are various

ways to type this punctuation mark, depending on the program being used.
- The function of parentheses is to enclose text, which, if excluded completely, would leave still a perfectly sound sentence.

UNIT 11: THE BAR (/)

Examples of usage:
1. I shall go next week on Tuesday and/or Wednesday.
2. Everybody should do his/her best to keep our streets free of litter.
3. On Sunday, the winner of the raffle will be announced and he/she will collect the prize.
4. I was born on 20/11/54.
5. At the end of the 2013/2014 football season, Cardiff City Football Club lost its place in the Premier League.
6. Whoever gets the job will be required to make his/her presence felt very quickly to raise the work ethic of the staff.
7. I shall buy a new desktop computer and/or a laptop.

Notes:
- All the following are alternative names for this mark: **diagonal**, **solidus**, **oblique**, **slash** and also, interestingly, the **virgule**, which was used, originally, to mean the comma.
- This mark is a **separator**, as the sentences suggest.
- Probably, the most used of the alternative names is now, because of computerisation, the **slash**.
- Apart from the uses illustrated by the sentences above, the bar is used also to mean **per** in expressions like: £30/hr.

UNIT 12: BRACKETS (( ))

Examples of usage:
1. I've been away with the family in my old car (on its last legs) on a week's tour of the Lake District.
2. Joe and Harry (my old mates) are the new champions at the snooker club.
3. Tuesday next (my birthday) I'm going on a cruise.
4. What about going to the theatre (where we met twenty years ago) and seeing them performing one of our favourite shows?
5. The sun is shining (at long last) and now we can cut the lawn.

Notes:
- Brackets are **separators**, as the sentences reveal.
- There are four types of brackets: **angle brackets**, **square brackets**, **brace brackets** and **round brackets**, of which the **round brackets**, used here, are the most popular.
- The uses of the other three types of brackets are not in keeping with the requirements of this particular study pack.
- Like the dash and the comma, when used in pairs, the brackets function as parentheses.
- In addition to the way the brackets are used in the sentences above, consider the following: You can expect me next Monday (July 10) at about 5.30 p.m.

UNIT 13: THE AMPERSAND (&)

Examples of usage:
1. I used to have an account with Bradford & Bingley many years ago.
2. We enjoy shopping at Marks & Spencer.

Notes:
- This symbol, which is not really a punctuation mark, is included because it is encountered fairly regularly in script.
- The ampersand is used today mainly in business names and is reasonably popular because of its appeal – being attractive – and the fact that it is space-saving.
- The symbol has been used since medieval times, when it was used in manuscripts, and was especially popular in the nineteenth century.
- Ampersand is a corruption of **'and per se and'**, meaning **'and by itself and'**.

UNIT 14: THE CARET (^)

Examples of usage:
1. January is generally the coldest month ^*of* the year.

2. Please reply with your suggested date for our ^*next* meeting.

Notes:
- The caret is used to indicate that there is an omission in the text and comes from the Latin **caret** meaning '**there is missing**'.
- As shown in the examples above, the practice is to insert the mark in the place where the missing word(s) should be and to write the word(s) immediately above the mark.
- The need for the caret has declined with the increased use of the computer, which arrests the attention of the typist when the text does not make sense.

UNIT 15: THE QUOTATION MARKS (' ')

Examples of usage:
1. 'I must go to the shop to get some fruit and vegetables for the weekend,' she said.
2. 'What's for lunch?' he asked.
3. He raised his glass and, in a loud and drunken voice, said, 'Good health!'
4. Looking very sadly at the coffin, John murmured, 'We were the best of friends and I'll never forget the day he shook my hand and said, "You and I are like brothers and always will be," but now he's gone!'
5. I was looking at the sky and thinking, 'Is it going to be sunny on this very special day, my wedding day?'
6. 'I think you're right,' I said, 'but not all the time!'
7. 'It was an evening like this that he asked, "Will you marry me?" I couldn't say no knowing that he'd already bought the ring.'
8. 'Since you said it would match your new shoes,' he said, 'why didn't you buy the new dress?' he asked.
9. 'Stop!' she shouted, as she saw the little boy running towards the deep end of the pool. Then, when he stopped and turned his head towards her, she added, in a much softer voice, 'Now, come here, please!'
10. 'Merry Christmas!' he shouted and, before anybody could reply, he started to sing very loudly and out of

tune, completely unaware of the fact that it was the middle of July.

Notes:
- There are two other terms for punctuation marks used, as here, for **direct speech**, being **quotes** and **inverted commas**.
- There is a need to differentiate between **direct speech**, which needs the punctuation marks featured here, and so-called **reported speech**, which is not shrouded in quotation marks. The following is an example of reported speech: He said that he was coming.
- It is important to respect that although an **utterance** can often be a sentence, this is not always the case. A common error in punctuating **direct speech** arises from the question mark and the exclamation mark being regarded as the same as a full stop in this regard.
- It should be noticed, in fact, that the two marks in question are treated more like commas than full stops in speech.
- Careful study of the sentences used as examples will highlight the fact that there are instances where **capital letters**, although probably expected, have not been used. Consider, for instance, sentences 8, 9 and 10 and notice that '**he**', '**she**' and '**he**' – the speakers – are all in lower case. This is because the sentences were incomplete, in each case, at the close of the speech – although the **utterances** were complete. For instance, in the case of sentence 9, the **utterance** ends with the exclamation mark – whilst the sentence ends with the full stop after the word '**pool**'.
- It will be noticed that **direct speech** is enclosed in a pair of quotation marks, but in addition there are

two versions of them – one pair features single marks and the other double marks. In the UK the single marks are preferred with double marks being used for **quotations within quotations**, as shown in sentences 4 and 7. In the United States of America, the opposite uses are common.

- In sentence 7, it will have been noticed that the word '**no**' was featured in the middle of a sentence without punctuation and in lower case. This is the correct way to introduce '**yes**' or '**no**' into text.

FINALLY!

Test yourself by correcting the punctuation of the following:
1. Saturday is my favourite day of the week
2. Sometimes I feel very tired at the end of the working week
3. When youre shopping will you buy me a new pen.
4. easter is a special occasion for all Christians
5. stop teasing the dog
6. "I shall leave about ten: "He said.
7. Lets have a cup of tea and some toast for breakfast today
8. He said that hell be here very soon and so will his wife
9. he was rude to me when he said you are an idiot and so I slapped him
10. foreign visitors especially Americans are always welcome in great Britain
11. In the Summer we are going on holiday to the South of france.
12. 'Hurry up please' he said pushing me on to the bus.
13. Tomorrow at about mid-day were going to see our grand-children
14. "How about a day at the races," He asked.
15. I have to say that I was surprised he said 'Yes' to the invitation, he admitted.

Corrected versions:
1. Saturday is my favourite day of the week.
2. Sometimes, I feel very tired at the end of the working week.
3. When you're shopping, will you buy me a new pen?
4. Easter is a special occasion for all Christians.
5. Stop teasing the dog!
6. 'I shall leave about ten,' he said.
7. Let's have a cup of tea and some toast for breakfast today.
8. He said that he'll be here very soon and so will his wife.
9. He was rude to me when he said, 'You are an idiot!' And so, I slapped him.
10. Foreign visitors, especially Americans, are always welcome in Great Britain.
11. In the summer, we are going on holiday to the south of France.
12. 'Hurry up, please,' he said, pushing me on to the bus.
13. Tomorrow, at about midday, we're hoping to see our grandchildren.
14. 'How about a day at the races?' he asked.
15. 'I have to say that I was surprised he said yes to the invitation,' he admitted.

Congratulations!

You've finished the course and, hopefully, it has proved to be, as promised at the outset, an *easier way* to achieve reasonable proficiency in the use of the main punctuation marks.